Landmark
Events in
American
History

The Anasazi Culture at
Mesa Verde

Dale Anderson

WORLD ALMANAC® LIBRARY

Please visit our web site at: www.worldalmanaclibrary.com
For a free color catalog describing World Almanac® Library's list of high-quality
books and multimedia programs, call 1-800-848-2928 (USA) or 1-800-387-3178
(Canada). World Almanac® Library's fax: (414) 332-3567.

Library of Congress Cataloging-in-Publication Data

Anderson, Dale, 1953-
    The Anasazi culture at Mesa Verde / by Dale Anderson.
      p. cm. — (Landmark events in American history)
    Includes bibliographical references and index.
    Summary: Discusses the civilization of the Anasazi people, who farmed the land
of Mesa Verdi, a plateau in southwest Colorado, around 550 A.D. and dug their
homes in the cliffs.
    ISBN 0-8368-5371-7 (lib. bdg.)
    ISBN 0-8368-5399-7 (softcover)
    1. Pueblo Indians—Colorado—Mesa Verde National Park—Antiquities—Juvenile
literature. 2. Pueblo Indians—Colorado—Mesa Verde National Park—History—
Juvenile literature. 3. Cliff dwellings—Colorado—Mesa Verde National Park—
Juvenile literature. 4. Mesa Verde National Park (Colo.)—Antiquities—Juvenile
literature. [1. Pueblo Indians—Antiquities. 2. Indians of North America—
Southwest, New—Antiquities. 3. Cliff dwellers—Southwest, New. 4. Cliff
dwellings—Southwest, New. 5. Mesa Verde National Park (Colo.) 6. Southwest,
New—Antiquities.] I. Title. II. Series.
E99.P9A5335   2003
978.8'27—dc21   2002036024

First published in 2003 by
World Almanac® Library
330 West Olive Street, Suite 100
Milwaukee, WI 53212 USA

Copyright © 2003 by World Almanac® Library.

Produced by Discovery Books
Editor: Sabrina Crewe
Designer and page production: Sabine Beaupré
Photo researcher: Sabrina Crewe
Maps and diagrams: Stefan Chabluk
World Almanac® Library editorial direction: Mark J. Sachner
World Almanac® Library art direction: Tammy Gruenewald
World Almanac® Library production: Jessica Yanke

Photo credits: Corbis: cover, pp. 4, 6, 7, 8, 9, 10 (both), 13, 14, 15, 16, 17, 18, 19, 21,
22, 23, 24, 25, 26 (both), 27, 28–29, 30, 31, 32, 33, 34, 35, 36, 37, 39, 40, 41, 42, 43;
National Park Service: pp. 20 (both), 38.

Printed in the United States of America

1 2 3 4 5 6 7 8 9 07 06 05 04 03

Contents

Introduction

Mesa Verde covers about 120 square miles (310 square kilometers). In places, the mesa rises over 2,000 feet (600 meters) above the land surrounding it.

The southwestern United States is a rugged land of mountains and **plateaus**. Wind and water have cut the red rock there into the most spectacular shapes. The climate is that of the desert, with little rainfall, and not much can grow in the area.

What Is Mesa Verde?

In the southwestern corner of Colorado, Mesa Verde rises above the surrounding landscape. Its name, from two Spanish words, describes it perfectly. A *mesa*—Spanish for "table"—is a plateau. In

The Four Corners

Mesa Verde is found in a part of the United States called the Four Corners. The region surrounds the point where the borders of four states—Colorado, Utah, Arizona, and New Mexico—meet. It is the only place in the United States where four states join in this way, and a concrete marker decorated with the seals of each state marks the spot.

the midst of the dry Southwest, this mesa stands out because it is covered by a carpet of green trees, mostly juniper and low pines, known as piñons. *Verde* is Spanish for "green," and so the plateau got the name Mesa Verde. The mesa is actually made up of several smaller mesas because it is broken up by river and stream valleys.

Who Were the Anasazi?

The region where Mesa Verde is located has some of the most beautiful scenery in the country. It is also home to many Native Americans. The greenery was what originally attracted Native Americans to the mesa. About 1,450 years ago, around A.D. 550, some of the Anasazi people in the area began living and farming on Mesa Verde. They thrived there for the next seven or eight hundred years, until about A.D. 1300.

Living on Mesa Verde

The first people to settle on the mesa lived in houses dug into the earth. Later, they built houses on top of the mesa, joining together the homes of many families in clusters known as **pueblos**. Still later, they built the most impressive structures found on the mesa —towns that were placed on the sheer sides of the cliffs that plunge down from the mesa top. The cliff towns held many houses and other buildings, such as storage rooms and ceremonial chambers.

Nearly four thousand separate sites on Mesa Verde contain remains of the Anasazi's lives. By studying these remains, scientists have learned how the ancient people of Mesa Verde lived. They are among the most important records of ancient American history that exist today.

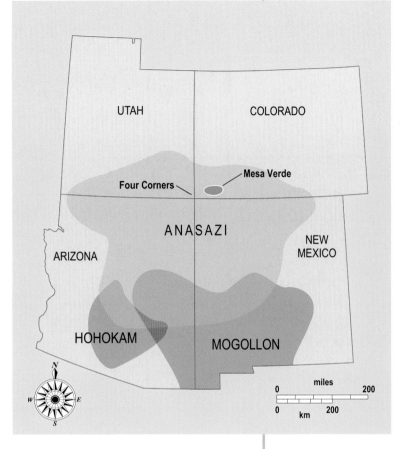

This map shows the area of the United States known as the Southwest. Mesa Verde is in the Four Corners region that was home to the ancient Anasazi people.

The Early Anasazi

Before they acquired farming skills, the Native people of the Southwest lived on wild foods, such as the fruit of the **yucca** plant, shown here in bloom. The yucca plant's purple fruit is similar to a banana.

The First Americans

The first people came to the Americas thousands of years ago. Many scientists believe they got there by walking from Asia to Alaska. At the time, vast sheets of ice covered large areas in the northern parts of the world. During this Ice Age, as the period is called, the level of the oceans was lower than it is now. A landmass may have connected eastern Asia to Alaska the Bering Strait, now a stretch of water.

If the first immigrants to America crossed this land bridge sometime between twelve thousand and eighty thousand years ago, they were probably hunters following the trail of large animals that they depended on for food. Over time, people spread across the Americas, settling every region from northernmost Canada to the southernmost tip of South America.

Reaching the Southwest

Around twelve thousand years ago, the first people began to live in the Southwest. They survived by hunting bison, or buffalo, among other animals, attacking their prey with spears with sharp stone points. As well as game, they ate any plant foods—nuts, seeds, fruits, and leaves—they could gather. The Native people of the Southwest moved from place to place within their own regions, following the buffalo herds and living in small bands of just a few people. They followed this way of life for thousands of years.

People of the Southwest

Other Native American groups developed and lived in the Southwest at about the same time as the Anasazi. The Hohokam lived in the harsh deserts of southern Arizona, and the Mogollon occupied what is now southern New Mexico. These peoples were

These spearheads were used by Mogollon people for hunting game. The Mogollon of southern New Mexico brought new ideas to the Anasazi from cultures in Mexico and farther south.

important to the story of the Anasazi. Being farther south, they were in contact with the civilizations of Mexico that were in turn south of them. Through Hohokam and Mogollon people, the Anasazi learned of and adopted some **technological** advances from Mexico.

An Accidental Find

The first evidence of the ancient hunters of the Southwest appeared purely by chance. In 1908, a former slave from Texas named George McJunkin was riding on the ranch he managed in Folsom, New Mexico. He found a bone sticking out of the earth that was larger than those of any animal he had ever seen. After McJunkin's death in 1922, the bone ended up in the hands of scientists. They realized that it belonged to a giant bison more than ten thousand years old. An expedition to the original site found the bones of twenty-three giant bison, and something even more revealing. In with the bones were stone spear points that had been used by the people who had hunted these animals. Named "Folsom points," they were unmistakable evidence that humans had lived in the area thousands of years before.

The Name of the Anasazi

The name Anasazi was coined by the Navajo people who came to the Southwest later. Anasazi means "ancient one" or perhaps "ancient enemy." The **descendants** of the Anasazi—Pueblo peoples such as the Hopi and Zuñi—do not have a name in their own languages for their Anasazi ancestors and so refer to them as the Ancestral Puebloans.

The Arrival of Farming

In the dry climate of the Southwest, plant-gathering was not a dependable source of food because few plants grow easily without rain. While people of the Southwest foraged for wild plants, Native people in central Mexico had found a more reliable alternative. They had been growing crops, especially corn, for a few thousand years. Slowly, over time, the knowledge of farming and a sturdy breed of corn worked its way north, first reaching the Southwest between 2000 and 1500 B.C. Some southwestern groups began introducing farming into their cultures. As well as corn, they introduced breeds of squash from Central America.

Corn grows in desert conditions in Arizona. The first people started farming corn in the Southwest as early as four thousand years ago.

The people now known as the Anasazi did not begin farming until later, around 500 B.C. Even then, they did not become full-time farmers and continued to hunt and to gather wild plant foods. They lived in natural shelters cut into high walls of rock, where a family or two would settle for a season. They might farm the land and then, after the harvest was finished, move to a new area.

Over time, however, farming became a more important part of Anasazi life. Anasazis began to settle down in one spot and stay for more than a year. Corn and squash became a larger part of their diet.

A Farmer's View of His Crops

"When a person planted corn, they would be raising these corn plants up as their children. We were taught to sing to our corn, sing to our children, talk to our children, to love our children, to care for them. Corn provides us with food. It is the center of life and the essence of life. Our ceremonies are prayers for rain in order that our corn will grow. When we plant corn or when we plant melons or squash or beans, we are showing our faith in life."

Ramson Lomatewama, a farmer of the Zuñi people, descendants of the Anasazi

The early Native Americans of the Southwest lived in caves in cliffs and under overhanging rocks. This cave in the Cedar Mesa area of southwestern Utah formed a natural dwelling for Anasazi people.

How the Early Anasazi Lived

The earliest of the Anasazi people wore few clothes in the warm summers of the Southwest. In the chilly winter, they covered themselves with blankets made of rabbit fur or of the stiff leaves of the yucca plant. They wore sandals made of yucca fibers year-round to protect their feet from the rocky terrain.

The Anasazi also wove beautiful baskets, using willow or other plants. They stored food in these baskets and coated their insides with **pitch** to make them watertight for carrying and storing water. People even cooked with these baskets. They did this by placing water and food inside and then dropping fire-heated stones into the mixture to cook it.

These sandals were made of yucca fibers. They were worn by Anasazi people who lived thousands of years ago.

The Basketmakers became skillful weavers who decorated their baskets with lovely woven designs.

10

Periods of Anasazi Culture

Historians and **archaeologists** divide Anasazi culture into different periods. There are two main phases: the Basketmaker period and the Pueblo period. Each period is further divided into smaller units:

1000 B.C.	**Ancestors of Anasazi** live by hunting and gathering.
500 B.C.	**Early Anasazi** begin to farm.
100 B.C.–A.D. 400	**Basketmaker period**: farming corn and squash; hunting and gathering.
400–700	**Late Basketmaker period**: growing beans; making **pottery**; living in houses dug into the ground; first settlement on top of Mesa Verde.
700–1100	**Early Pueblo period**: using bow and arrow; living in houses built above ground; widespread settlement on Mesa Verde.
1100–1300	**Classic Pueblo period**: Anasazi spread to largest area; cliffside towns on Mesa Verde.
1300–1600	**Late Pueblo period**: Mesa Verde is abandoned.

The Basketmaker period gets its name from the intricate baskets that the Anasazi made during those earlier centuries. The name *Pueblo* is based on the apartment-like housing that the Anasazi built to make their villages and towns during the later periods. *Pueblo*, in Spanish, means "town," and it was the Spanish that first gave that name to the dwellings of the Southwest.

Chapter 2

On Top of the Mesa

Up to the Mesa

When the Anasazi began to farm seriously, the green landscape of Mesa Verde must have seemed attractive to those in the immediate area. If trees could flourish there, they might have wondered, why couldn't corn and squash? Sometime around A.D. 550 or so—in the Late Basketmaker period—a number of Anasazi people climbed from the valley below to the top of Mesa Verde and began to farm.

A Wise Choice

The Anasazi made a wise choice in settling on the mesa. It was a good place to farm for several reasons. The land rises 2,400 feet (730 m) above the valley floor at its highest point in the north. Because of this, the mesa top is cooler in summer than the valley below. In the winter, however, the sun reaches more of the mesa than it does the valleys, which are often covered in shadow. As a

The Anasazi people inhabited many areas of Mesa Verde. This map shows the sites of some of the main ruins. The names of the sites were given to the places after they were rediscovered in the nineteenth or twentieth centuries.

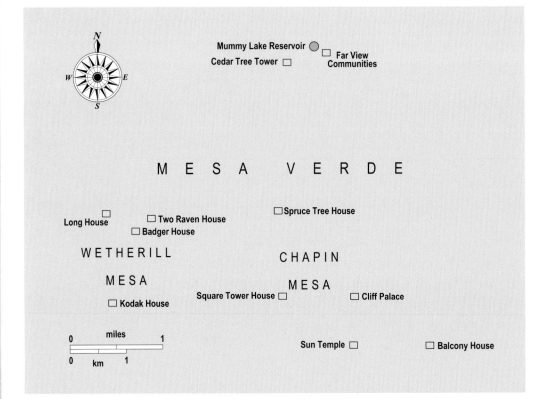

Snow on Mesa Verde was a valuable asset to the Anasazi when it melted in the spring and could be collected for irrigation. In this photograph, the ruin of the Square Tower settlement can be seen nestling below the mesa in the side of the cliff.

result, the mesa is somewhat warmer than the lowlands in winter.

While Mesa Verde is high at its northern end, it slopes down to the south, presenting its face to the sun's warmth. This makes for a long growing season. In addition, the mesa receives more moisture than do the nearby lowlands. Much of this falls as snow during the winter, but heavy rains fall in the late summer as well. Mesa Verde also has springs that provide water.

The winds that blow over the mesa cover it with good soil. The mesa top was more fertile than many of the lowland areas because of this soil, and its fields were more productive than those down below. The many trees growing there provided a valuable supply of wood, which was scarce in the dry lowlands. This wood could be used to build structures, to make tools, and to serve as fuel for fires.

Why the Anasazi Climbed the Mesa

"Much of the southern Colorado Plateau was unfit for growing corn. Even the best areas were marginal. Land lying below 5,500 feet [1,700 m] was too dry, and land above 7,500 feet [2,300 m] was too cold. Even with the narrow belt suitable for corn, local **droughts** and frosts struck frequently. As a result, the Anasazi constantly were moving, looking for areas of favorable rainfall and temperature."

Kenneth L. Petersen, archaeologist, talking about the problems facing Anasazi farmers

An intact example of a large Anasazi cooking pot. Pots replaced baskets at the end of the Basketmaker Period and could be used over open fires.

New Technology

Around A.D. 550, about the same time that they moved onto the mesa, the Anasazi adopted some important new technology. As with farming, these advances came from the south and reached the Anasazi through contact with the Mogollon people. One advance was the bow and arrow, which made hunting more efficient.

Another useful innovation was pottery. The Anasazi began to make mugs, pots, and other vessels by coiling clay. When the clay dried, the object could be used to store food or water. Since pots—unlike baskets—would not burn in the campfire, the Anasazi could use them for cooking and could cook their food more thoroughly. Pottery replaced baskets for most uses.

New Resources

The Anasazi began to grow beans, another crop imported from the south. Beans provide protein, which was valuable when meat was scarce. Beans had an extra benefit. They put nutrients back in the soil. These nutrients aided in the growth of corn planted there the next growing season. Likewise, the corn left the soil in good shape for beans, and so the two crops could be rotated to good effect.

In the Basketmaker period, the Anasazi had dogs for pets and to help hunt. In the Late Basketmaker period, they tamed wild turkeys. These birds were valued for their feathers. Women plucked the feathers and tied them together with yucca fibers to make coats and blankets. Some historians think they turned from fur to turkey feathers because rabbits had become scarce from too much hunting.

Traditional Resources

The Anasazi in this period also continued to rely on the resources that their people had used for centuries. They hunted deer and prairie dogs. They collected nuts from the mesa's piñon trees. The nuts were roasted or ground up into meal, or coarse flour. The Anasazi also ate the banana-like fruit of the yucca and the fruit of the prickly pear cactus. They used yucca fibers for their sandals and some of their clothing.

Their lives were changing, however. The corn, beans, and squash they grew became their main food sources, and pottery gave them a range of useful utensils.

Turkey Troubles

"Before long [the turkeys] had added a lot more than anyone bargained for—stalking the roads and tying up traffic, raiding the gardens of staff residents, moving onto porches at the visitor center during [bad] weather and refusing to leave. They stole food, crowded inside houses when doors were left ajar, and worst of all, they [dropped dung] on everything."

Donald Pike, writing about an ill-fated attempt by the National Park Service to bring turkeys back to Mesa Verde, Anasazi: Ancient People of the Rock, *1974*

A wild turkey in the Arizona desert. The Anasazi people farmed turkeys for their feathers and their meat.

The interior of this restored **kiva** at the Spruce Tree House site on Mesa Verde gives visitors an idea of what early pithouses were like. Residents used a wooden ladder to climb in and out. Recesses in the walls were used for storage.

A New Kind of Home

One of the biggest changes in Anasazi life was in their dwellings. In earlier times, the Anasazi had lived in rock shelters provided by nature. Now they began to build their own houses. These early structures are called pithouses because they were dug into the ground.

Using stone and wooden tools, the Anasazi dug pits 3 to 5 feet (1 to 2 m) deep, creating a large circular area anywhere from 9 to 25 feet (3 to 8 m) across. They lined the inside with flat stones, as they had done with storage chambers in cave dwellings.

To make a roof, people cut four small tree trunks and stuck them in the base of the pit, near the walls, to make a square. Then they lashed other tree trunks across the top to form a supporting frame. Next, they placed tree limbs over the frame to fill in the roof. The limbs were covered with twigs, bark, leaves, and grasses, and then the whole roof was coated with several inches of dirt.

A hole in the center of the roof was used to get into and out of the house by ladder. It also served as a smoke hole, letting smoke from the fire escape. Other, smaller openings in the roof let in fresh air.

People living in pithouses used part of the main area for cooking and the rest of the space for sleeping. Two smaller pits were dug on one side and connected to the main chamber. They were used to store food and other supplies.

Living Together

The pithouses were an improvement over living in drafty, cold rock shelters, but they could be very dangerous. The fire needed for warmth and cooking could easily ignite the roof, which was only a few feet above the floor. Many of the remains of pithouses show signs that they had caught fire at some time.

There was another difference between the rock shelters and the pithouses. In the past, just one or two families occupied a rock shelter. With the new pithouses and a greater food supply from farming, more and more people could settle in the same area. It was at this point that the Anasazi began to live together in small communities. Villages with as many as fifty pithouses have been found.

In the Pithouse

"An individual pithouse was occupied for an average of about fifteen years. By modern standards . . . these early [homes] of the Anasazi were cramped, smelly, crude, dark, smoky, and cold most of the time during the winter, but probably far superior to the caves and temporary shelters [they] were used to."

Manitou Cliff Dwellings web site

Pithouses were built in groups as these kivas were at Pueblo Bonito, an Anasazi settlement in Chaco Canyon, New Mexico. Acquiring building skills led the Anasazi to begin living in communities.

The Far View community shows how extensive above-ground communities could be. Far View was occupied from around 900 to 1300 and includes nearly fifty pueblos within a half square mile (1.3 square km). The number of homes suggests the community was home to hundreds of people at any given time.

The Pueblo Period

Around 750, near the beginning of what is called the Early Pueblo period, the Anasazi made another major change in housing. The dark, underground pithouses made of earth, wood, and bark were replaced by houses built above the ground.

The first structures were made by sticking wooden poles close together in the ground, like a wood fence, and covering them with mud, which hardened in the sun to form a solid wall. To support these walls, the Anasazi builders placed stones along the base.

Later, people simply built the entire walls out of stone. At first, these were rough stones piled on top of each other and held together with large amounts of mud **mortar**. As time passed and their **masonry** skills improved, the Anasazi began to use stones that were carefully cut and shaped to be even and fit together well.

Flattened Heads

The backs of people's skulls from the Early Pueblo period are flattened rather than rounded. Scientists believe this was caused by a child-rearing method of that time. In earlier times, Anasazi mothers used a soft padded cradle to hold young babies. Around 750, they began to use a hard wooden board, to which they securely tied their babies so they would not fall while the women worked. Because babies' skulls are soft and easily shaped, the hard board flattened the backs of their heads. As the skull bones hardened, they kept this shape.

When the walls were finished, they were covered with a thin layer of plaster made from mud. After the mud dried, the inside walls were often painted and given other decorations. Roofs were similar to those made for the pithouses: large beams were covered with smaller poles and then branches, and the whole thing then covered with mud.

The First Pueblos

Several of these new, above-ground homes were joined together to make small villages, or pueblos. They were joined at first in a line and later in shapes resembling the letters L, E, and U. By 1100, masonry skills had developed to the point where people could make larger, more complex buildings. Builders made two rows of stone so that the walls would be strong enough to hold a second story of houses on top of the lower level. They also extended rooms forward on the ground floor, using the additions for living space and the back rooms for storage.

Separate families lived in each home, but the Anasazi on Mesa Verde were living in increasingly large groups. This could have been for defense against invaders. At about the same time, people were beginning to seal up windows and doors lower down and to build houses with no openings at all at ground level.

Stonework by Anasazi masons still looks very impressive after hundreds of years. It is even more so when you think that they had no machinery and used the most basic tools to cut and fit stone.

Life Among the Anasazi

In the 900s, the Anasazi dug a large reservoir (right) in the Far View area. It was mostly for domestic needs, but a channel also sent water to the fields for irrigation. Below is a natural spring on Mesa Verde.

By today's standards, life for the Anasazi was hard. They worked with tools of stone, bone, or wood and lived in a difficult environment with little rain. Despite these difficulties, the Anasazi created a lively culture and raised enough food to feed as many as five thousand people when the Mesa Verde population was at its height.

Precious Water

People worked carefully to make use of every drop of water—none was wasted. Collecting water was crucial. In the spring, when the winter snows melted, the mesa people collected water in large pottery jars and stored it in cool places for use later in the year. They also found the natural springs on Mesa Verde and made basins of stone to catch water that seeped through the rock. Women collected this water in jars and brought it back to their homes.

Watering the Crops

Anasazi men used technology to water their crops. They selected the best spots for farming—areas where the water naturally runs. They also built dams on the mesa tops to hold rainwater or snowmelt. The farmers then carefully positioned a few rocks to channel water where they wanted it. These irrigation methods expanded the area of land that could be farmed.

Anasazi planting methods were designed to retain water in the soil. Farmers made holes for seeds with wooden digging sticks. They planted a few seeds of corn in one spot and then moved a foot (0.3 m) or more away before planting the next seeds. Over each group of seeds, they raised a high mound of dirt so that the soil would hold its moisture for as long as possible through the dry summer.

Surviving the Dry Months

"Every effort is made to conserve the water supply, for as the warm weather continues the springs begin to dwindle and the pools shrink. There is no repairing and building of houses; water cannot be spared for the mortar. Pottery is seldom made at this time for that, too, requires water. By using it only for human needs the supply can be drawn out for months if necessary."

Don Watson, Indians of the Mesa Verde

One the many things the Anasazi used their pots for was to store water collected from melted snow, occasional rain, or natural springs. This water storage jar was typical in its design, with a narrow neck to prevent evaporation.

Today in the Southwest, Pueblo Indians such as this Hopi farmer still farm corn under desert conditions, much as the Anasazi, or Ancestral Puebloans, did before them.

Daily Work

Men did most of the farm work. In the spring, they cleared the land, using fires to fell the larger trees and stone axes to bring down smaller plants. All summer long, they tended the fields, pulling weeds to make sure that these invaders did not steal precious water from their crops.

Young boys and older men watched the fields, making sure that animals did not eat the crop. In the fall, at harvest time, everyone helped. Men, boys, and children harvested the crops. Women shucked the corn and freed the beans from their pods. Anyone who could carried the food back to the village. The best ears of corn were stored to provide seed for the next year's crop.

Women gathered nuts, berries, and other wild plant foods. They used stones to grind the corn and cooked the cornmeal in liquid. They also prepared the meat brought back by hunters, butchering the game and then stewing or roasting it.

Anasazi society

Scientists believe that the Anasazi—like the Native Americans who live in the Southwest today—had a matrilineal society. That means that children belonged to their mother's family and traced their descent through their mother. When a young man and woman married, the couple built a new home near the woman's family.

Pottery Making

It was the women who made the pottery, the remains of which have taught us so much about Anasazi life. They coiled long ribbons of clay into the shape of a platter, bowl, jug, or mug, and then smoothed the surface to remove the ridges made by the coils.

The earliest pottery was not decorated, but over time the Anasazi began to paint their pots. After drying the pot in the sun, the women added a white clay coating and painted a design with paint-brushes made out of long, thin yucca fibers. The paint, made from the juice of the beeweed plant, was brown, but it turned black when the pot was placed in the fire for its final hardening. The distinctive designs of Anasazi black-on-white pottery are still admired today.

An Anasazi pottery mug, ladle, and grain storage jar. In the background is the Spruce Tree House cliff dwelling.

Among Southwestern peoples today, it is women who own property. This may have been the case among the Anasazi too. If so, the men who worked the farms were not farming their own land, but the land of their wives.

Families were part of clans, a group of families that claimed a common ancestor. Husbands and wives belonged to different clans and children belonged only to their mother's clan. Each clan adopted an animal, such as the badger or the turtle, as its symbol. Clans played an important role in Anasazi spiritual life.

Spiritual Life

Pithouses did not disappear completely when the Anasazi began building above-ground houses. They still built underground, but the structures were no longer used as homes. They were *kivas*, a word from the language of the Hopi people of the present-day Southwest. Kivas today are chambers where spiritual ceremonies are held. The Anasazi structures strongly resemble those still used by peoples of the Southwest, which is why historians think that the ancient kivas had spiritual purposes.

The kivas were not exactly like pithouses. They were built of stone, not simply dug out of the ground and given crude wooden roofs. They were much larger than the original pithouses—as big as 60 feet (20 m) across. People sat on stone benches around the inner wall.

There were similarities to the pithouses, however. People entered kivas through the roof; the fireplace was in the center; and shafts on the side allowed fresh air to enter. If the ancient kivas were used in the same way as modern ones, only men would have been allowed inside, and each clan would have had its own kiva.

The great kiva at Pueblo Bonito, shown here, would have been a gathering place for people from many clans, all of whom would have had their own clan kivas as well. You can see the round hole of the sipapu in the foreground. Originally, the kiva would have had a roof over it as all kivas and pithouses did.

These are **petroglyphs** that were found in Navajo Canyon on Mesa Verde. The images show people, animals, and spirals that may represent the movement of the Sun. They could have had spiritual meaning or simply be records of hunting triumphs, good harvests, or conflicts.

Like modern kivas, the ancient ones had a hole in the floor called a *sipapu*. Historians think the sipapu reflects Native American stories of the creation of humans, which say that humans were born inside the Earth and reached the surface by crawling through a hole in the ground.

A Southwestern Creation Story

"In the beginning two female human beings were born. There was land already, but no one knows how long it existed. The two girls were born underground at a place called Cipapu. There was no light. . . . [The spirit] said, 'You have the seeds of four types of trees. Plant them; you will use the trees to climb up.' . . . A certain pine grew faster than the others, and after a very long while it pushed a hole through the earth and let in a little light.

"A shaft of light now reached into the place where the two sisters lived. 'It is time for you to go out,' [the spirit] said. 'When you come to the top, wait for the sun to rise. . . . Pray to the sun . . . with pollen and sacred cornmeal, which you will find in your baskets. Thank it for bringing you to the light. Ask for long life and happiness, and for success in the purpose for which you were created.'"

Creation story of the Ácoma people of New Mexico, American Indian Myths and Legends

Moving to the Cliffs

The existence of trade networks among Native American groups led to the exchange of crafts, skills, and goods over large areas. Anasazi goods, such as these earrings (right) and shell beads (below), were traded with other peoples.

Reaching a Peak

Around 900, the Anasazi culture began to reach its height. Anasazi communities covered a larger area and held more people than ever before. Their stonework showed great skill and their pottery great artistry.

Well-built roads cut straight across the Four Corners region, connecting many Anasazi villages. Traders brought luxuries like the bright feathers of macaws from Mexico or shiny seashells from coastal communities. They carried cotton from the drier southern areas to the north, where it did not grow very well. They took turquoise and pottery from central New Mexico to trade in other areas.

Rumblings of Trouble

There were problems, however. Some parts of the Four Corners were struck by severe droughts in the 1100s. Some areas had lost their trees, which damaged farming. Once the trees were gone, wind and water could wash good soil away.

Chaco Canyon was not only an important center of Anasazi culture, but the hub of a large trading network spanning many other Native communities. In the foreground of this photo are the remains of Pueblo Bonito, the biggest Anasazi community in Chaco Canyon.

In some areas—including Mesa Verde—the Anasazi began to build towers that reached 10 to 15 feet (3 to 5 m) high. They could have been watchtowers and part of a warning system. An Anasazi lookout in one village who spotted a threat could signal to another village to raise the alarm. This and other evidence suggest that fighting was on the increase in Anasazi country, either because other people were coming into the area or because different groups of Anasazi were fighting among themselves.

The End of the Chaco Settlements

More evidence of these troubles is seen in the collapse of settlements at Chaco Canyon in northern New Mexico. From about 900 to 1100, Chaco culture had great influence on other settlements. In the 1100s, however, its hold on other Anasazi groups started to weaken. By 1200, Chaco Canyon itself—once home to more than five thousand people—was completely abandoned.

Impressive Work

"Pueblo Bonito was at the hub of Chaco [Canyon], the axis from which the roadways emanated, and in many respects it represents the most sophisticated architecture in the pre-Columbian United States. During many previous visits, wandering inside the ruin, I had stared in awe at some of the finest masonry crafted in the prehistoric Southwest: tabular slabs of sandstone, often thinner than my little finger, shaped and fitted so tight that I could not see the mortar that bound them together."

David Roberts, "The Old Ones of the Southwest," National Geographic, *1996*

Cliff Palace is the largest Anasazi cliff dwelling site found on Mesa Verde. It had more than 200 rooms and 23 kivas. The cave holding Cliff Palace is more than 320 feet (98 m) long, nearly 90 feet (27 m) deep, and almost 60 feet (18 m) high.

The Cliff Towns

Anasazi culture on Mesa Verde reached its peak somewhat later than other areas such as Chaco Canyon. At the time that Chaco was declining in the 1100s, the Mesa Verde people were moving into larger communities and their masonry and pottery were growing more sophisticated. In the 1200s, however, the people of Mesa Verde abruptly made yet another change in their homes. Many of them left the mesa top and began to build their homes in the cliffs that formed the sides of the mesas making up Mesa Verde. The cliffs have many caves large enough to hold buildings and whole villages.

Most of these cliffside settlements were small and had homes for only a few families, but some were large and spectacular. Long House had about 150 rooms and 21 kivas. Spruce Tree House had nearly 120 rooms and 8 kivas.

Up and Down the Cliffs

There is no record to tell us why the Anasazi made their move to the cliffs. Whatever the reason, however, living on the cliffs created challenges. Historians think the Anasazi did not have any paths leading to the mesa tops or the canyon bottoms. The only way they could move to and from the cliff towns was by climbing up or down the sheer face of the cliff. Even today, the finger and toeholds that

the Anasazi cut into the cliff face can still be seen. Their skill at rock climbing appears even more impressive when you realize that they had to climb in this way while hauling food and supplies into their towns. Children and older people tended to stay close to home because the climb up from the cliffside home was risky.

Why Did They Move to the Cliffs?

Why did the Mesa Verde people move into cliff dwellings? No one knows. Some historians say the move reflects the problems that were bothering the whole Anasazi region in these years. Living in the sides of the cliffs, they say, gave the Anasazi protection from their enemies.

Others think that the move to the cliffs was a sign of environmental problems or of a growing population that increased the demand for food. By moving homes off the mesa tops, the Anasazi were leaving more land there to be farmed. Some researchers point out that if the Anasazi had fields both on the mesa tops and the canyon bottoms, living on the cliffs put them closer to both areas.

The cliffside villages offered some climate-related benefits. The winter wind can blow very cold over the mesa top, but the cliff towns were protected from this chilly air. The overhanging cliffs also shielded people and their houses from rain and snow.

At Long House, these buildings were fitted right into the back of the cave to use as much of the available space as possible. Surrounding these existing walls would have been other walls and other rooms, and the whole space would have been very crowded.

Living in the Cliffside

Life on the cliffs was a little different from that on the mesa top. Conditions were probably crowded, since there was little space in a cliff site that did not contain buildings. The dwellings in the cliffs were built in the same way as they had been on top of the mesa, but now people had to carry building materials up and down the cliffs.

Cooking was not done inside the homes but outside, on top of adjacent roofs. The homes had no windows and only one small doorway, so cooking inside would have filled the room with smoke. Some historians think that cliff dwellers did not build warming fires inside their homes for the same reason.

Rooms in the back of the town were used to store food to last the winter. Seed for corn and other crops to plant the following year were stored there as well. The tamed turkeys were allowed to walk through the town during the day, but at night they were collected into empty spaces at the back.

Taking Out the Trash

Garbage was a problem in the confined area of the cliff dwellings. One dump site was any open space between the backs of the buildings and the inner wall of the cave; another was the area in front of the village. Archaeologists digging in the piles of debris in front of cliff buildings have found sandals, broken pottery, tools made of bone or stone, corncobs, and countless other leftovers of Anasazi life. They have also found dead bodies, buried in dump sites because the heaps of trash were easier to dig into than the surrounding rock.

Anasazi debris found at Eagle Nest cliff dwelling in Lion Canyon, Colorado.

Health in the Cliff Dwellings

Conditions in the cliff towns, as in the rest of the world at the time, were not very sanitary. Some rooms toward the back of the towns were apparently used as toilets. These conditions might have led to increased sickness as disease would spread easily with lack of hygiene in a closed space.

Many Anasazi bodies that have been found show evidence of suffering from arthritis. Tooth problems were common, too. Cornmeal ground with stone was rough and gritty, and eating it wore away at the tough enamel coating people's teeth, causing cavities and infections. Historians believe that those Anasazi who survived early childhood died by their fifties from sickness, wounds, or infections for which they had no cure.

What Happened to the Anasazi?

Remnants of ancient life have been found at abandoned settlements on Mesa Verde and elsewhere in the Four Corners region. This shell necklace is an example of Anasazi craftsmanship found hundreds of years after it was made.

Walking Away

"There is that easy flow through life. Build up this community, something happens, time to go, move on to the next place, leaving the pot sitting there, walking away from it, without any need to pack it and take all your possessions with you. The thing that you took with you was creative capability, and that was all you needed."

Rina Swentzell, a writer from Santa Clara Pueblo, quoted in Stephen Trimble, The People, 1993

Leaving the Mesa

In the late 1200s or early 1300s, the Anasazi suddenly left Mesa Verde and much of the northern and western parts of the Four Corners region. They simply abandoned their pueblos, including the impressive cliffside towns that had been so difficult to build.

The Anasazi not only left their homes, but they left many possessions behind. The first people to explore the cliff towns in the late 1800s found numerous pieces of pottery, yucca sandals, jewelry, and other items.

Many historians note that the Anasazi had a history of moving from one place to another when the land was no longer productive. To this day, no one knows exactly why they left Mesa Verde, but everyone agrees that the climate was a major problem for the Anasazi in these years. Scientists believe that the harvests of the early 1270s were plentiful. In 1276, however, little snow or rain fell, and the crops did not thrive. The same thing happened the next year, and the year after, and the year after that. By 1300, Mesa Verde had suffered more than twenty years of drought.

Square Tower House, with its impressive four-story tower, was one of many cliff dwellings that was suddenly abandoned by the Anasazi people of the Mesa Verde.

Where Did They Go?

The first European Americans who learned about the Anasazi thought that they had disappeared or died off. They also thought that the people who had built the stone towns and cliff dwellings were more advanced than other Native Americans who lived in the Southwest at the time.

This idea lasted for many years, but no one believes it now. Modern archaeologists recognize that the Anasazi lived in many more parts of the Four Corners region than Mesa Verde alone. They believe that the people of Mesa Verde— along with those from other northern parts of this region— simply moved south. There they settled on other mesas and other lands. Many of them settled in the valley formed by the upper reaches of the Rio Grande in present-day New Mexico. Others settled in western New Mexico or eastern Arizona.

The traditional culture of the Ácoma people of western New Mexico shares much with that of the Anasazi, and the two cultures are probably connected. This is Ácoma Pueblo in the early twentieth century.

A Boom in the South

"The speed of the buildup was breathtaking. About A.D. 1300 three families moved into an area above a spring and founded Arroyo Hondo [a site near what is now Santa Fe, New Mexico]. Within thirty years the population had soared to fifteen hundred. The same happened all along this stretch of the [Rio Grande]. Had more of these Anasazi built with stone instead of mud, the Rio Grande would be lined with dramatic ruins."

Dr. Douglas W. Schwartz, archaeologist, who studies the resettlement of the Anasazi

The Pueblo People

"Pueblo Indians" is a collective name first used for people of the Southwest by the Europeans who settled in the region long after the Anasazi. Today, most historians agree that some Pueblo Indians of Arizona and New Mexico are the descendants of the Anasazi who moved south in the late 1200s and early 1300s. The Pueblo peoples live in apartment-like pueblos similar to those of the Anasazi. They farm using some of the same methods as the Anasazi. Their kivas are similar to the ancient kivas of Mesa Verde and other Anasazi sites.

The modern Pueblo people feel a deep connection to the ancient Anasazi. As one Zuñi man says, "The Anasazi are well and happy in the Rio Grande valley."

There are some mysteries, however. One of the biggest is that of language. If the Pueblo peoples were all the descendants of the Anasazi, they would be expected to speak the same language, or at least similar ones. But that is not the case. Some Pueblo languages are related to one another, but not all of them.

Contact with Europeans

In the late 1500s and early 1600s, Spanish explorers came to the Southwest. The Pueblo people came into contact with white people for the first time. This contact threatened their very survival.

The Spaniards tried to conquer the Pueblo peoples, and this effort led to resistance and fighting. Some groups were wiped out in these fights. Other groups died out, as they did all over North America, because they became exposed to European diseases against which they had no natural defenses. Conflict and disease took a terrible toll on the Pueblo peoples. When the Spaniards arrived, there were more than eighty Pueblo groups. Today, there are only twenty-two groups.

The homes of the Pueblo peoples are made of **adobe**, or dried mud, rather than of the stone used by the Anasazi, but they are still built in the pueblo style. Taos Pueblo, New Mexico, shown here, has been continuously inhabited for about seven hundred years.

This fine turquoise and silver jewelry was made by a Zuñi craftsman. In the background is a Catholic cross, a reminder of the Spanish influence in the Southwest.

Changing and Staying the Same

Contact with Europeans changed the Pueblo peoples' lives in other ways. They began to grow new crops brought from Europe, such as wheat. They acquired herds of livestock. Another change was in religion, as many Pueblo people accepted Christianity. Even today, however, they keep alive ancient and traditional religious beliefs. Like other Americans, they have accepted modern clothing and technology, but the Pueblo people are unusual in the way they have succeeded in sustaining their culture.

Each Pueblo group lives in a certain area. Most of these home bases, such as Taos Pueblo, are near the northern Rio Grande in New Mexico. Three—those of the Ácoma, the Laguna, and the Zuñi—are in western New Mexico. The areas where the Hopi live are in eastern Arizona.

In these places, people follow many traditional ways of life. Some pueblos have become famous for their arts. The Hopis make beautiful sculptures of carved, painted wood, called Kachina dolls, that represent ceremonial religious figures. Artists from several pueblos are well-known for their lovely, hand-crafted pottery. Even today—as in the ancient Anasazi times—these artists use yucca leaves to paint intricate designs on their pots.

At a ceremony in Taos Pueblo, dancers wear traditional feathered costumes. Pueblo people are known for their dances.

Chapter 6

Digging into the Past

Discovery

After 1300, no one lived in the Anasazi pueblos on Mesa Verde. The buildings sat in stillness. Over the years, weather damaged them. The roofs of kivas and pithouses collapsed, and the pits filled in with dirt. Winds knocked down stones that had once formed the walls of houses. What had been flourishing towns became ruins. Trees and shrubs once more grew across the mesa top, covering those areas that had been farmland. The sites remained unknown, at least to European Americans, for hundreds of years.

Richard Wetherill (c. 1860—1910)

Richard Wetherill was the oldest of five Wetherill sons and the most devoted to looking for Anasazi artifacts. The Wetherills sold what they found to collectors, but from the beginning, Richard Wetherill kept notes on where and how objects were found, hoping that scholars could learn from this information. It was he who discovered the first evidence of the Basketmakers and named that period of Anasazi history.

Wetherill wished to do this work "in such a manner that anyone in the future cannot pick flaws in it." That wish was not fulfilled. Some see him as a gifted amateur archaeologist, but others complain that he robbed the sites of many objects. They say that, through sloppy work, Wetherill destroyed clues that other archaeologists could have used to learn about the past. Whether Wetherill was a hero or a villain, he put Mesa Verde on the map. And the objects he and his brothers dug up are displayed in several museums.

A basket from the Basketmaker period is uncovered during excavations in Colorado. It had lain unseen for fifteen hundred to two thousand years.

In the late 1880s, members of the Wetherill family were tending their cattle in the canyons below Mesa Verde. A Ute man named Acowitz, who lived in the area, had told them of amazing ruins on the mesa's cliffs. He said the Ute people were afraid of the ruins because they contained the spirits of the people who had lived there.

In the winter of 1888, two members of the Wetherill family spotted a number of cliffside towns. Investigating, they found many **artifacts** and some of the **mummified** remains of dead people. They named several of these sites—names that are still used today—and collected some of the objects they found.

Finding Out About the Anasazi

The Anasazi did not write their history in books. How, then, do we know so much about them? The use of stone tools, pottery, turkey-feather robes, and other matters of everyday life can all be revealed by finding these objects, or fragments of them, in the ancient homes. Bones at campsites reveal which animals the Anasazi hunted and ate. The remains of corncobs show that they ate corn, which they had to farm because corn does not grow wild.

Unearthing an Anasazi pot, as this archaeologist is doing in Arizona, is a rare and exciting occurrence today. Most sites have already been excavated and have had their treasures removed.

To find these objects, archaeologists cannot use picks and shovels to dig—these heavy tools might destroy the very things they are looking for. They have to dig carefully and slowly with small tools.

Few artifacts of Anasazi life remain at Mesa Verde today. Archaeologists may find broken bits of pottery or flakes chipped off pieces of stone by Anasazi who were making arrows. When they are very lucky, they find an entire bowl or water jug.

Date Detectives

How do scientists know how old these artifacts are? In some cases, objects are found in layers. The farther down a layer is, the older the objects in that layer are. This method does not tell scientists exactly what year an objects dates from, however. They need a more precise form of evidence for that, and that evidence is wood.

Each year that a tree grows, its trunk gets wider. The year's growth is shown in a ring that can be seen when the tree is cut down. Scientists can take a sample of wood found from an Anasazi site and, by looking at the pattern of its rings, say what year that tree was cut down. That information helps scientists tell how old each Anasazi site is. They have matched samples of wood taken from across the area, and this has enabled them to construct a history that reaches hundreds of years into the past.

Tree rings provide another important piece of information. They reveal how much rain fell in any year in the past. When rain was plentiful, the trees grew a great deal, and the rings from those years are wide. In years of little rain, though, these rings are very narrow and close together. By studying these rings, scientists have identified the many years of drought in the late 1200s.

Ancient Treasure

"The blood sang in my head. In that small, special space between the tilting slabs was a basket, placed facedown. On a glance I saw that it was as perfectly preserved as any museum specimen and that it was a classic Basketmaker . . . container. Dull tan in color, made of either willow or yucca fiber, woven in so exquisitely tight a pattern I knew it would hold water, the basket evidently lay where someone had left it . . . fifteen hundred years ago."

David Roberts, In Search of the Old Ones, *1996*

Tree ring samples from a giant sequoia help this scientist understand the tree's history. By studying the tree's rings, he can determine the amount of rainfall at different times in the tree's life, as well as how many fires the tree has survived. This science is called dendrochronology.

Conclusion

A National Treasure

In 1906, a large part of Mesa Verde was made into a national park. It was the first park created in the United States to preserve archaeological sites. At the park are displays showing arts and crafts of Pueblo peoples today and a museum with exhibits that tell the story of the Anasazi and their way of life. The park also stores many artifacts that have been recovered from different sites. Archaeologists who are studying the Anasazi can examine these objects as they try to test their ideas about the past.

Thousands of visitors come to the park each year. The mesa offers magnificent views of the Four Corners region. On a clear day, you can see the stunning shapes that wind, water, and time have cut into the rock.

On the mesa top, visitors can walk through such major sites as Far View and the Sun Temple. They can also see some of the spectacular cliffside sites. Visitors to ancient towns, such as Cliff Palace, Long House, and Spruce Tree House, can see the handiwork of the Anasazi and imagine what life was like on these precarious rocks hundreds of years ago.

The Anasazi settlement of Balcony House is just as hard to reach as it was two thousand years ago. Visitors use ladders installed by Mesa Verde National Park to reach the site.

Fire Damage

Two huge fires swept across the mesa top in the dry summer of 2000. The first, the huge Bircher Fire, did no damage to any known archaeological sites. The second, the Pony Fire, burned up some park facilities and damaged some sites.

In the dry summer of 2002, a lightning strike started another large fire at Mesa Verde. Known as the Long Mesa Fire, it lasted from July 29 to August 5 and spread over an area the size of 2,500 football fields. The fire damaged five National Park structures but did not harm any known ancient sites. It took 376 firefighters, 37 engines and pumpers, 5 helicopters, and some timely rain to put the fire out.

Helicopters carrying water go to and from the Bircher Fire, dropping their loads on the flames. The fire burned up a band of vegetation 8 miles (13 km) long and 4 miles (6.5 km) wide.

The Legacy of Mesa Verde

The legacy of the Anasazi people of Mesa Verde is most apparent in the lives of the Pueblo people who are their descendants. The modern Pueblos still farm the same harsh, dry land that the Anasazi once farmed. The religion of the Puebloans also reflects the lives of the Anasazi. People belong to clans, and clan members meet in kivas, just as in the past. Even the ruins of the Anasazis' ancient homes have a tale to tell. Their now-silent towns and villages reveal that a hardy and resourceful people with strong communities once flourished in a beautiful but difficult environment.

Time Line

500 B.C.	Anasazi begin to farm.
100 B.C.	Beginning of Basketmaker period: farming corn and squash plus hunting and gathering.
A.D. **400**	Beginning of Late Basketmaker period: farming beans, making pottery, making pithouses.
550	Anasazi begin to settle on Mesa Verde.
700	Beginning of Early Pueblo period: using bow and arrow, building above-ground houses.
900	First settlements are built at Far View community. Far View reservoir is built. Kivas begin to appear on Mesa Verde.
1200	Chaco Canyon is abandoned by Anasazi. Anasazi on Mesa Verde begin building homes on cliffside sites.
1276	First of many years of severe drought on Mesa Verde.
1300	Mesa Verde is abandoned.
1540s	Spanish first reach the Southwest.
1888	Wetherills find Cliff Palace and other sites.
1906	Most of Mesa Verde is named a national park.
1936	Term "Anasazi" replaces the older term "Cliff Dwellers."

Glossary

adobe: building material made of mud mixed with straw and dried in the sun.

archaeologists: people who study remains of earlier human cultures.

artifact: something made by humans and still existing from an earlier time.

descendants: people who come in a later generation in a family. This could be grandchildren or people many generations and hundreds of years later.

droughts: periods with much less rainfall than normal, causing shortages of water for growing plants and for human and animal consumption.

kiva: stone pit structure built by the Pueblo peoples for spiritual purposes. Today's kivas probably derive from earlier ones built by the Anasazi people, which in turn derive from the even earlier Anasazi pithouses.

masonry: stonework. A person who is skilled in stonework is called a mason.

mortar: paste used in stonework that hardens when it dries to hold stone in place. The mortar used by the Anasazi was clay and water mixed to make mud.

mummified: preserved by a drying out process. The mummification of a human body can occur naturally if the body is left in a dry enough place.

petroglyphs: manmade carvings, usually consisting of images, in a rock surface.

pitch: thick liquid obtained from the sap of some trees. If pitch is spread over a surface and left to dry, it will make the surface waterproof.

plateaus: raised areas of land with a fairly level surface.

pottery: type of object such as a bowl, drinking vessel, or container made by shaping moist clay and then using heat to dry it so that the clay becomes hard and keeps its shape.

pueblos: Spanish word for "towns." In the Southwest it refers to the apartment-like clustered towns of the Native people. "Pueblo Indians" is the collective name given to various groups of Native people living in the Southwest.

technological: having to do with technology, the knowledge and ability that improve ways of doing practical things.

yucca: plant occurring in the Southwest that has a long, thick stem with long, stiff leaves around the base and a cluster of flowers at the top.

Further Information

Books

Goodman, Susan E. *Stones, Bones, and Petroglyphs: Digging into Southwest Archaeology*. Atheneum, 1998.

Hausman, Gerald. *Turtle Dream: Collected Stories from the Hopi, Navajo, Pueblo and Havasupai People*. Mariposa, 1989.

Rasmussen, R. Kent. *Pueblo* (Native American Homes). Rourke, 2001.

Sita, Lisa. *Indians of the Southwest: Traditions, History, Legends, and Life*. Gareth Stevens, 2001.

Warren, Scott. *Cities in the Sand: The Ancient Civilizations of the Southwest*. Chronicle Books, 1992.

Young, Robert. *A Personal Tour of Mesa Verde* (How It Was). Lerner, 1999.

Web Sites

www.cliffdwellingsmuseum.com/anasazi Good information about the Anasazi people from web site of the Manitou Cliff Dwellings.

www.co.blm.gov/ahc/artifact.htm Anasazi Heritage Center displays ancient artifacts from Mesa Verde and other Anasazi sites.

www.nps.gov/meve/ Mesa Verde National Park offers practical information about the park and the Anasazi sites to be found there.

Useful Addresses

Mesa Verde National Park
P.O. Box 8
Mesa Verde, CO 81330
Telephone: (970) 529-4465

Anasazi Heritage Center
27501 Highway 184
Dolores, CO 81323
Telephone: (970) 882-4811

Index

Page numbers in *italics* indicate maps and diagrams. Page numbers in **bold** indicate other illustrations.